His Noble Numbers

George Klawitter

iUniverse, Inc.
Bloomington

His Noble Numbers

The views expressed in this work are solely those of the author and do not necessarily reflect the views of the publisher, and the publisher hereby disclaims any responsibility for them.

iUniverse books may be ordered through booksellers or by contacting:

iUniverse
1663 Liberty Drive
Bloomington, IN 47403
www.iuniverse.com
1-800-Authors (1-800-288-4677)

Because of the dynamic nature of the Internet, any Web addresses or links contained in this book may have changed since publication and may no longer be valid.

Any people depicted in stock imagery provided by Thinkstock are models, and such images are being used for illustrative purposes only.

Certain stock imagery © Thinkstock.

ISBN: 978-1-4502-9033-3 (sc)
ISBN: 978-1-4502-9034-0 (ebk)

Printed in the United States of America

iUniverse rev. date: 1/26/2011

for

Alan Altimont

The man whose silent dayes
in harmeles joyes are spent,
whome hopes cannot delude,
nor sorrow discontent,

that man needes neither towers
nor armour for defence,
nor secret vautes to flie
from thunders violence.

Hee onely can behold
with unafrighted eyes
the horrours of the deepe,
and terrours of the Skies.

—Thomas Campion

Acknowledgements

"Art Responds to Artist" in *Touchstone*
"Descent" in *Visions International*
"In the Garden" in *Touchstone*
"Kill to Shoot" in *Texas Poetry Calendar*
"Mr. Angus Mitchell" in *Sorin Oak Review*
"The Randy Telephone Man" in *Très di-verse-city*
"Justin" in *Borderlands*
"Dog Gone" in *Sorin Oak Review*
"Passage" in *2010 Texas Poetry Calendar*
"Carnival Animals" in *Texas Carnival Glass Newsletter*

Other Poetry Books by George Klawitter

Country Matters
The Colt
Let Orpheus Take Your Hand
The Agony of Words

To His Book

Who with thy leaves shall wipe (at need)
The place, where swelling Piles do breed:
May every Ill, that bites, or smarts,
Perplexe him in his hinder-parts.

—Robert Herrick

Contents

Backyard Drama

The neighbors sneer, but she's defiant,
continues to feed the raccoon nightly,
the possum, and the rabid lonely fox
who show up darkly apologetic, sick for love.

That's when the moon shimmers everything
in soft, romantic light. No such theater
in full sun when all the birds appear,
the wren and sparrow, cardinal, and jay.

At noon comes her favorite rogue, the one
who stopped an August day to steal her heart—
a road runner, skinny as a twig and mindless
in his dominance of the molting yard.

She didn't mind the occasional finch he ate,
but one brown afternoon he grabbed a prize,
the only parakeet, and bashed its beady head
on the flat patio rocks, beat it dead.

She ran for her broom, but the rogue-bird
flew its bounty to a neighbor's eave
to eat in peace and spit green feathers
on the tearful matron down below.

Funny how abuse comes home to roost.
Her tightened heart tries to forgive,
but the dainty thrust of hate will not let go.
She glowers every time the brat arrives for lunch.

No wild parakeets have filtered lately to her yard—
word gets around. She daily shovels
scraps and seeds into bottomless feeders
for grateful ones unaware they could be next.

Garcia

When his grandfather shot himself,
Garcia didn't drop a tear, not one.
The image of the old man sucking
on the barrel didn't register
inside Garcia's brain, not then, not now.

But the ashen bullet ripped clean
through the old man's cerebellum,
shattering every dream Garcia sang
whenever blood and flesh arranged itself
inside his doughy lump of heart.

Garcia moves in squares: his dancing eyes
reflect the films he's never made.
But hopes green up in youth
no matter what a grandfather exacted
from a clay decision gone to pot.

As seasons go, Garcia swims through
expectations, hitting meaning in his days
while somewhere back in Mexico on a ranch
an old man's memory is fusing into rock
and mesquite where iguana like to pass.

Descent

When her husband tipped into the hell
some researchers have tidied up
by giving it a scientific name,
she sacrificed her life to enter his.

Her sketches went unsketched,
her poems rocked in utero, and everywhere
the stink of promise festered in her brain
as his ground down into a whisper.

One day she came into the kitchen
where he gnawed raw chicken:
"I was hungry," he explained.
She waited desperate for salmonella.

Then music he had loved became abhorrent.
He screamed in pain, "No, no, no!"
with covered ears. So she cancelled
Mahler, Bach, Vivaldi from his desiccating soul.

The man who'd thrilled to Shostakovich
froze in terror when he couldn't process all the notes
that flew in fury at his disappearing nerves
as the calm of night washed him backward into innocence.

Wonders Will Never Cease

They've opened up a horseshoe made of glass
beyond the canyon rim some twenty feet
from where the Colorado carved its coffin
fifty million years ago. The river
then was king, made up its own mind
how and where to dig the regal trench
and decorated it with rings of gold, maroon,
purple, mauve, green, and turquoise blue.

Today it dribbles at the base so far beneath
our tourist eyes we don't concern ourselves
with it unless, of course, we swing its rapids
in a rubber boat—then we taste its anger,
still the grandfather of conquest biting rage
into the rock and dirt. But most of us just
leave it down near hell, stay so far away
it has no meaning as we spit into the great abyss.

Here's this ugly thing of glass, protruding
where it was never ever meant to be,
but some deadly guy of capital believed it
god-given to turn a buck off the beauty
Mother Nature can't appreciate.
Men and women drag their kids and dogs
into the quaint contraption looking down.
Some pray, some scream, some vomit.

I wonder what the noble native dense with dignity
would think about this silly monster.
After all, his gentle body, swathed in deerskin,
rested simply at the canyon lip and watched the sun
do magic cartwheels on the ragged walls below.
He never questioned why, never twisted purpose.
Or am I wrong? Did he sit and muse that he could turn
some wampum by erecting a glass horseshoe here?

The Rothko Chapel

When I saw the Rothko Chapel
I didn't understand
I was supposed to sit
on wooden benches and stare for hours
at huge canvases of black black black.

I gave a quick look at all the walls
and wandered back into the foyer
where I was tempted to reach
into the fishbowl for my dollar
still floating there,

but the Medusa at the door
kept her eye on me as if she
half expected me to dip into the dish
and maybe take a little extra
for my loss of a good afternoon.

Later when I learned
that there were colors hidden
in the black, I wanted to return
and live inside those massive things,
swim inside the wine dark seas,

rush into the depths of hell,
where Rothko lived just
months before he ended it
inside the darkness of his soul,
with all his bleakness bled

to these chapel walls
where we're supposed to take
a little bit away each time
we live the rich and subtle shades
of purple, red, magenta,

until the white of hope
fuses with the black of hope
and all is one with us
inside the Rothko chapel
in Houston, Texas.

Trueblood

He claims he's Sioux. I don't know. I search
his face for evidence of tribal war,
his hands for scars, his arms for broken arrow,
his soul for rapture in a cause sublime.

But smeared across the residue of crime
from government, society, and church,
he rises noble in the dawn before
the sun affords him elegance of sorrow.

He knows the past but cannot know tomorrow
ticking near in reservation time.
No law degree, no poetry, research,
or job can right an ancient score.

His total joy, his happiness, is more
than what blond hair and his blue eyes can borrow.
Underneath his native skin, design
and darkness ripple, touch to kiss, and merge.

Years After

On a sea of hope no deeper than
a Cajun bayou, New Orleans floats.
The images endure:

convicts squatting at the end
of a broken highway, its concrete stump
rising from the murky water

while the great sun boils.
If the hurricane had never visited,
the nightmare might suddenly fade.

Yet bodies float by, bags of skin,
rotting flesh bloated by the heat—
they bump into the pilings aimless

as the heart of a city sunk into
the cemeteries, its music
silent but for the occasional shout

"Is anybody in there?" sung into attics
from a dozen makeshift barges
navigating watered streets.

The silence stiffens—no birds
because the trees are gone.
Nowhere to roost. No rainbow in the sky,

just ugly death on its holiday,
an early eerie Mardi Gras
along the parade route down to hell,

the hospitals aghast, the airport dumb,
nothing but the not-so-secret cry of Despair
stuttering by the dead, putting pennies on their eyes.

Wool Gathering

I sneak into Walmart late at night
to feed my latest hobby: crochet.
As luck would have it, the aisle for yarn
is next to Automotive.
Go figure.

So while the macho men are fingering lug nuts,
I'm loading my arms with skeins of wool:
canary yellow, passion pink, and amethyst.
I stammer loudly, "Damn the little woman—
makin' me buy her friggin' yarn."

Then I scrunch along the side aisle,
weave my way through shampoo, condoms,
and cosmetics, choose an empty check-out,
plunk down my wool and eye
the short Hispanic gal behind the counter.

"How pretty, " she says.
"I have a thing for color," I volunteer.
She smiles. I decide to bare it:
"I could lie and tell you these are for my wife,
but I don't have a wife."

She giggles and I go for broke:
"When my mother was alive,
she wouldn't teach me.
She always said, 'Men don't crochet.'
But now she's gone, and I can do whatever I want."

The woman sombers and points a finger up:
"Your mother's there
looking down on you."
I clutch my bag of guilt and leave,
heavy again with truth and dare.

Final Day

for Kate Frost

When she touches wood for the last time
and lets the chalk slip between her fingers
to the floor, she knows retrieval is
a futile exercise. These brittle brains

in front of her will grow from crime to crime
without her harried cries, and so she lingers
as they leave for other worlds, the quiz
from yesterday as valueless as trains

departing without passengers across
her eyes blurred by blond and black and red—
her favorite colors. Now she flips the light

to off and gathers things. No more the boss,
she's tinsel in the corridor, this heart that bled
for kids who run fast past her left and right.

Family Confession

I punish the way my mother would, motherly,
because my father was a silent witness
assenting to the various tortures she devised
to keep the house like apple pie, each slice in line.

My brother bucked so he was out, pariah,
before his brothers' sleepy eyes could know his lie,
his sister too much into growing up to notice
his quick evaporation much beyond the hurt.

We thought we didn't mind the empty space at meals,
but somewhere in the heavy air between the discipline
our mother threw and the soft paternal yes,
my brother's absence waxed our adolescent throats.

We settled into tense routine, and art flourished:
a yellow plastic radio spun opera out on Saturdays
across the kitchen to the ironing board while a piano played
its necessary chords, and charmed lives sneaked away outdoors.

Kill to Shoot

Sous-gardener, he doesn't call the shots:
someone says, "Plant this juniper," he plants it.
"Prune the bougainvillea," he prunes,
knowing she's the happier for the trim.

He props the jasmine, culls forget-me-nots,
all on cue, as he understands it,
sequencing the Master Plan. Moon-
flowers grace his nights and daisies bless him.

But when the order came to drop the pair
of pomegranate trees blooming orange
inside the campus quad, he took his saw

and spent the morning cutting through their hair,
every rip a wrench of manly courage.
And as his sisters fell, his heart was twisted raw.

Fingers

Underneath the Sorin Oak
I told him that his fingers,
thin as drinking straws,
were made to play an oboe.

Then in the darkened coffee shop
I saw his lightning on the frets
and knew those fingers found
a home away from woodwind,

as they flew up and down
the comely neck of his guitar
lit only by some strings
of rainbow lights and tinsel.

Some would say he came to us
from the Garden of Adonis
where babies wait in beds of roses
to drop and quicken empty bodies.

So in the campus moonlight
when I pass beneath the massive oak,
his fingers haunt me, dancing
as they do across the belly

and the graceful neck
of anyone becoming music
pulsing underneath
his gentle probing.

Cemeteries

The Steger cemetery satisfies because its trees
give permanence to a changing Midwest town,
oaks and maples reaching fingers down,
caressing vaults and caskets in the earth.

Sassafras maneuver bones, suck the DNA
abruptly into sunshine, laughing
at a new cortege arriving with a load
of fresh protein-manure.

It's all about recycling, and the farmers
know the sooner that they turn a profit,
the sooner can the wife get laid.
The trees are partners in this ancient game.

On the other hand, the cemetery
ripe at Saulges grows with a cornfield
carved from its ruptured side.
Nothing inside the place but stones

that root so slowly you have to wait
a million years for them to sink their teeth
into the dead awaiting resurrection
on this dusty road in rural France.

Reborn through quartz, the bodies here will rise
up gently in the early morning mist
so much the stronger for their tardiness.
No gully wash will knock them to the sea.

Justin

He told me that his father beat him once,
only once, years ago. A boy of ten when
his father snapped, the fists flew like dominoes
while a paper mother blanched in fear,
and every angel in the house flew for cover.

He told me all of this inside the comforts
of my cluttered office when I shut the door.
All the books on all the shelves listened
knowing that within their own spiny pages
violence splintered into awkward deeps of pain.

He told me that the single nasty incident
never came again, but I suspect the dreams
of childhood are visited forever and the rush
of horror never leaves us even when we reconcile,
one victim to another, awash in guilt and grief.

He told me life continues, like the sudden pauses
in the sad expensive ship that Breughel sailed
past Icarus. So that's my boy—the only leg
we see is perfect. We have to guess at teenage lungs
gasping through the green of water calling, "Father! Father!"

Professor Angus Mitchell

That dour Scotsman hasn't come
to campus yet. He always waits
until the weather's right—

no reason to brave sunshine
when a soaking rain is healthier.
He thrives inside a fog.

Now he sports a sprig of heather
in his sweet lapel, says everyone
should have a little heather here or home.

Of course he smells of boggy peat
and snarls there's never haggis
in the school cafeteria.

Overall we tolerate his bulk,
and some dim day we know he'll slip
along the sidewalk in his bonny kilt,

ignoring mirthful students,
to sell us all on gloom—
the only answer to a universe like ours.

Autumn Shakespeare

In Zilker Park after dark, a soft October
night with crickets in the soft folds
of the trees around us, children laughing,
the whirl of a sitar from a microphone.

José passes with a mega-bag of popcorn
from the bright concession stand,
joins his friends on blankets
where the hill slopes deepest to the stage.

A father stoops to ask what's going on:
the name *Midsummer Night's Dream*
registers with him, and so his family settles
for the spell of Oberon, Titania, and Puck.

An usher gives out programs,
but the print is small,
and the sun is all but gone.
Anyway, this play will sell itself.

Nearby, a couple on the grass
entwine, oblivious of Iraq
where the killing deserts run pink
with bloody sand and gunpowder.

I have a sophomore summoned off to fight.
The gentlest soul Louisiana sent us,
he's packing as I write. The war machine
won't let him finish the semester.

No, it needs him in the dirt.
At first it said, "Afghanistan."
But then another letter bounced along:
"Not Afghanistan but Iraq—and sorry for the typo."

Typo? I thought misspelling is a "typo."
How can you spell Iraq "Afghanistan"?
I'd like to send a typo to the White House:
"Washington? We meant Iraq. Pack and go."

The reply would most likely be:
"We have to get them before they get us."
I say if they want to live here, let them.
Wait—Theseus and Hippolyta approach.

Wisconsin Solo

Katie Dissmore played the trombone
in the local symphonette.
Who'd guess that she was eighty-two?

Not Frank the mailman who put her through her paces
every Saturday in the basement of First Lutheran
where the group met, barring blizzards.

She had played with Sousa once
when Sousa came to town.
Yes, she was quite a prodigy,

and even now when Katie takes a ride
into a long cadenza, Frank gets glassy-eyed,
as he remembers Sousa beaming too.

Her arms seem senseless here without a horn,
senseless and so tuneless on a satin mattress,
smothered under roses, ferns, carnations.

She was made for tougher rides,
slides into a quick fortissimo,
not this catafalque for beauty queens.

No doubt the trombones somewhere
bring an extra chair for her tonight
into their row beside the tympani.

Differences

When I bought the pot made
by a descendent of Cochise, I was told
the blackened smudges on the sides
were fire-clouds sent, I suppose,

by the God of the Plains to mark
this child in a special way, no two
alike, each smiling grimly to the past,
remembering lakes and trees and thunder.

Paul reacts with a different shade:
not fire-clouds, just burn marks bold
enough to catch the hum of bison hides
and rabbit fur, some of those rasping,

firing clay in a fired dark,
emerging from the ground kiln,
born anew to live a century or more,
the last reminder of a people ripped apart.

She seems so out of place,
bouncing light on my melodeon,
old beyond the ivory keys
and rosewood lies of parlor drama,

pioneer-chosen, Rafaelita's baby parked
atop a feathered doily, her hue
quiet against the infinite blast
for us who touch Cochise and wonder.

Passage

The berries burn red
on the tree outside
my office window.

Two blue jays flit
among the leaves.
They won't eat.

Only cedar waxwings
sate themselves
on the crimson drops.

I wait every year
for the flock of yellow
against cerise.

The feast takes all
of fifteen minutes or so.
Then I'll wait again in green.

The Trampoline at Midnight

So there's the trampoline and here he is
ready for the plastic web and rope.
Intimidated bones and skin
expect his visit with a sigh and tremble.
Isolated from the house it waits
for visitors since the little girl
who wanted it has moved to other wants.

So that leaves him, the long-time neighbor
who can sneak across the darkened yard
between the twisted oaks and cedars
to worship at the winsome god.
Night after night while we sleep our sleep,
he shucks his clothes beside the rain barrel
and walks across the cool moonlit grass.

One summersault—he's in or on
to hazard first a practice leap.
The creaking rubber slaps his feet
and tosses him airborne among the trees.
He's down, he's up, the breeze inside his hair,
his arms out wide, his frowzy balls knocking
at his rustic thighs, all bliss, all whim.

Never in his eighty odd deceptive years
was anything so fresh as this, no job,
no sex or sin ever quite so sweet.
The barest sounds of squeak and groan
curl out into the purple of the night.
He spins, he twirls, he lands upon his rump.
He joys in dance. He delicately erects.

With every heave toward heaven, he's
the envy of the critters in the somber yard.
They gather mute and reverential:
black-eyed raccoon, a slinky fox,
a possum quiet in his summer guilt,
and ringed around the old man's sweat,
come sweet cecropia and fire flies.

The patient spiders wait their turn,
the gopher and the garden snake.
The ox-eye daisies and the fretty chervil
bob and weave. How fair his fling!
The world can roll because the bouncing
never stops. To move, the universe
depends upon this ancient, solitary thing.

The Swan at Blarney

He dangles underneath the famous stone
and my wings flapping in the sullen breeze
while I, his agent provocateur, hold tight
with heavy webby feet and scaly yellow knees.

There is no squawk, just a gentle moan
as he stretches to endorse his right
to kiss the limestone green with Celtic moss,
smoothed around the edges to a gloss.

He fusses little at my bland request
to loosen as I ruffle skin for feather,
but once I'm in, he tightens to a squeal,

welcomes his new turgid summer guest.
We grasp the storm that gathers in his nether
world, then swirl above as church bells peal.

Texas Fall

The garden in its dying mode—
yellow-bells dropping night by night,
a blue-sky vine barely able
to lift a velvet head to meet

its life-long master, the sun,
that fickle lord who runs
his attention more and more
to other gardens miles away.

The Lady Baltimore attempts
to control the place with her daily
pink saucers, but almost casually
she sheds her fragile leaves.

They fall from bending stalks
to the hungry earth where worms
and fire ants await, eager
to ignore hibiscus pride.

No one doubts the bird-of-paradise
will return next year as regally
it crowns its fronds with final tries
at summer, art, and beauty.

Its orange is everywhere in stars
across the yard, and pods
of seeds balsam-brown spring
to every corner where there's room.

The honeysuckle nods in Roman grief,
its trumpets slipping into autumn,
that barbaric hound ready
to assume the precious reins of empire.

Only the sago palm refuses to give in,
continuing to stretch its darkened needles
into graying neighbors, knowing snow
will never freeze its royal throat.

Something has to subsist past death.
It may as well be this giant
with its all too sharp fingers poking
lost intruders who risk its space.

Anxious for the light and grateful for the rain,
it does not preen so much as raise
its rigid arms to accommodate
a massive heart that sobs the local loss of green.

Puzzle

Why did Nazis strip Bonhoeffer naked
before they marched him to the gallows
that April day in 1945?

Or did they order him to strip himself,
unwilling themselves to touch
his unsung clerical flesh?

Or did he request to be stripped
like his carpenter-god
so the two could be alike in death?

Or did he strip himself, willing
to be as Francis was—naked
in death as he was at birth?

He declared, after all, it was his birthday,
that glorious spring when he arose
from death to his redeeming heaven,

where he romps, nude and fresh,
beyond the glare of guns,
the hate of specious war.

The seraphim hardly notice him
so intent he is to blend into the choir,
alone at last in community.

He turns in light, eyeless,
noiseless, his triumphant questions
fused with wonder in his answers.

At the Delta

I don't like those seacoasts
where the land ends defiantly
and water begins. You know:
here I am, there it is.

Sure, the tide comes in daily
to grab a little dirt furtively
and then retreat back
to farm its algae kingdom.

That's just a game:
the gnarly ocean spits
as much sand in return
for its measly thefts.

No, give me the delta
where I can walk for hours,
never knowing if my pilgrim feet
are about to sink or float.

Let me stand where water
and land co-exist, puddle
nurtured by island, no one
knowing who is ruling whom.

I like to see the birds keep guessing
where to hunt for caterpillar
or water-creature, crawling
between death by drink or thirst.

I like to see the sun mystified
where to settle for the night,
nestling into dubious trees
or sloshing in a silvery grave.

The river that swims from
land to ocean controls this play.
The actors bob and weave
at its whimsy and command.

Everything at the delta moves
this way or that because the river
decides a path moment by moment,
every move a languid gesture.

So if there is a delta god,
he's protean—his landscape
slithers right before our eyes,
ensuring our amphibian surprise.

Dog Gone

Paul hasn't had a chance to cry just yet,
but grief will come to rip his waiting heart,
and tears, those magic beads of resignation,
will pour along his face and down his chest.

He'll never know the time. Perhaps he'll set
the dish beside the water bowl apart
from hers and catch himself too late, the ration
still so automatic for their nest,

and then the vision of the gentle one,
nudging close to get his share before
the lady nips his ear—all vanishes,

that nightly moaning and the daily run,
the nose for nuisance, appetite for sport—
just emptiness for joys it banishes.

A Flower's Ruse

I went out this morning to cut down
the Lady Baltimore but found
at one finger-end a large green bud

as if she knew I was on my way:
she muscled every inch of energy
to shove a final baby to the light.

Too sad—seeing her in autumn olive,
all the perky summer colors gone to earth,
a few leaves clinging to the matron stalk.

Oh well, winter will arrive, snow and all,
so let her have her final crazy days.
November sleep creeps in soon enough.

Leaving San Angelo

Tall as a pine and wise as a mother owl,
she came to life among the grandchildren
who listened to her poetry and marveled

at the way she sang into the words,
how she contoured images. Colors
rang through her verse, and sea shells,

and islands in the Pacific the youngsters
in denim around her would never see
except through her spoon-fed lies.

She wrote of anything and everything
with energy from lagoon-blue eyes,
vapored like a summer sky in June,

and never took back a line
once she knew it was perfect
for the universe.

Maternity

The insides of a woman—
fine strands of something
waiting to be braids.

You see them spin in love,
feel the filaments twist
into a pulsing heart.

What frustrates thread
we never know—divergence
from a motherhood or trauma—

but haywire, the spokes
break, jam, and jar,
ruined beyond fixing.

Madonna crumbles
toward eternity wondering
always what might have been.

Painters

When artists bury themselves in paint and frame,
they risk a loss of touch, the only gift
the gods left them scratching loveless on
the universal canvas we call earth.

Cantankerous worms, they struggle for a name,
sprouting eyes and ears, crossing drifts
to brain, creating voice, thrilling song,
standing upright, effecting their own birth.

Now we walk among their oily scenes,
their flowers frozen next to bowls of fruit,
their laughing ladies on their beaux-arts swings,

their naked boys cavorting, and it means
in art we've found reflection and the truth
of being gods by brushstroke, kings of things.

Heritage

My great-grandmother floats in time—
no photo, not even a first name:
maybe Julia, maybe Carolina.

Until a week ago I had never seen
a picture of her husband,
but now carved into my heart

all the dignity of his gentle face
stares at me above his Prussian uniform,
the buttons crisp as glass eyes.

Their son married the daughter
of a Slovenian cholera orphan,
a fierce embittered boy

who died softly in America,
having slipped his raucous genes
into my available body.

That man was a brute. He lies buried
on a green hillside in Illinois,
enjoying the sunshine and snow.

Meanwhile I work to reconcile my
appropriate heritage—feisty Slovenian brat
with gentle Prussian in the photo.

Wherever that soldier lies in Europe,
I hope someone will stumble across
his melting stone, push away the moss,

and find him quiet under a blue sky
in his handsome Prussian cerements
next to my anonymous great-grandmother.

The Life of a Professor

My life is very glamorous.
When I wake up, I beat
the maid just to get in shape.

Then while she scrubs my back
in my sumptuous bath,
I plan my scholarly day.

Over breakfast I complain about the eggs,
even if they are done to perfection,
just to let her know who's boss.

Then I'm off to my luxurious office
to be brilliant all day
and destroy some lives.

Back home she's out of tears
so a few more whacks
and then it's down to the filet mignon.

I keep her an hour overtime without pay.
Then she's gone, and I'm in bed
to swim my commodious dreams.

Streaks of Sadness

My cousin Barbara had it, and her brother John,
but not their sister Mary who laughed into the wind.

Since Mary was the oldest, maybe at her birth
she took all the happiness and left the shards for others,

bits of happiness, a little here for John,
a little there for Barbara—the rest into the wind.

Every piece of nature Mary took, she squeezed into herself,
then left it there, went on to something else.

Her brother and her sister got the parings,
did what they could with what was left behind.

They grabbed for leavings, shuddered at the universe,
held each other dear for scraps of what they gleaned.

A little knowledge for them both could stretch into eternity—
they pawed each bit for truth and ached when it would bite.

Any subject Mary didn't get, she tossed it off,
like unripe corn, a Judith in the Holofernes scene.

John and Barbara picked at it: there must be meaning
somewhere in it, somewhere in the cortex, in the phloem.

Mary had no time for truth since she herself was truth.
People came and went from her like flies:

some drank, some sneered, and most could never
understand just what it was that wound her clock.

She never settled into anything. A gypsy soul, she wandered,
insides stopped at noon, both dials fixed at twelve.

Barbara left for heaven early. John remained to chronicle
the likes of girls his world could never reconcile.

He captured streaks of sadness as he captured sound,
alone, the words all jumbled one against the other.

A Time for Answers

I want to be there at the mercy
of the weather, caught in the after-white
snow brings to trees and lanes,

the tremendous calm of cold
that dominates the world,
everything frozen to the sight,

and nothing moving but my feet
into the gentle thrill of winter,
real winter where the world

changes color,
brown things hibernate,
leaving all there is to wind and sky.

There a peace seeps deep
into me, my eyelids doors
to process the absolute stillness

of the forest, blank on blank,
footprints behind and nothing ahead
but adventure and wonder,

those sullen sisters brought to life,
reluctant to give out joy,
almost afraid of meaning,

tense the grief is gone,
sad the absence of routine
evaporates for dream.

The child goes out,
eighty years young,
the crunch of frost beneath his feet,

a few flakes dancing on his head
from branches overloaded
overnight.

This is no alien land,
no land unknown,
this the path that was meant to be,

manageable, full of answers,
simple ones,
every question dissipated into yes.

In the Boat

As he skims above the muddy fish
and brackish turtles, Gordon tames the water,
makes it answer to his muscle, swings
its greenish-blue to glimmer in the sun.

The morning smiles to his athletic wish
where the river's Nereid and her daughter
wait among the willows, their silver wings
pulsing the air, making the breezes hum

as if the sound of tartan pipes and drone
impel him solitary at his task.
He works the oars, his toes becomes a drum.

Blue herons rise, unruffled cygnets moan
behind the wake, their alabaster last
to break for the rowing man who comes.

Franciscan in the Ashes

for Mychal Judge

He's Francis now, gone home
where lilies always bloom
and skies emblue their silk,
where daffodils sing in rows
and angels bathe in light.

The rubble's gone to dust,
those buildings deep into the dirt,
brought down one New York morning—
what others couldn't waste below
some wasted from above.

He was there foot-sore,
coughing through the concrete soot,
sifting through the pain,
one finger in the holy oil,
another on a fevered brow.

Unlike the gentle going in a soft
Assisi garden, this trooper
went in horror, deadened by debris,
but his sorrow's history here:
he's Francis now, gone home.

November Gift

Marie brought weeds. She said
these autumn pods and stems would shore

my soul against the winter. Here I sit
a victim wrapped in milkweed silk

and queen anne's lace, my only joy
the subtle scent the wild carrot throws

around my brittle nose, a scent of fields
yielding to snow, a trace of mouse and beetle,

noisy cricket, sluggish larva entering cacoon,
a tortoise lumbering against the moon.

The Loneliness of the Hunt

He sits in the blind waiting for autumn dawn
to creep its way across the marshy reeds,
his only props a gun, metal-cold,
and a golden dog ready for the jump.

In quiet meditation he dreams among
the ghosts that people here, their ancient needs
for food and fur a common bond. He holds
communion with their dying logs and stumps.

A sudden stir. He cocks and watches where
a blur of grey and blue takes off across
a glimmer on the lake. He arcs above

and shoots, feeling along his chestnut hair
electric waves. His pal returns to toss
a carcass at his feet. This is love.

For a Favorite Niece

the lily sprouts
so slowly
in the spring

you hardly notice
the leafy fronds
before

her flower unfolds
a white so bright
you have to

shut
your
eyes

Peace Poem

It seems to me there are two ways
to write a poem about peace.

One way is to write about dancing
in a field of daffodils
where the sun always shines
and God has a house
just around the corner.

The other way is to write about gore
or the prospect of gore,

drag your audience through the violence
of people doing unspeakable things
to people they don't like
while their leaders vivisect
in the cranky halls of the U.N.

So here is my poem about peace.
Take it or leave it:

daffodils in Darfur,
lilies of the Afghan valley,
crocuses for Chechnya,
daisies fresh from Belfast,
poppies dancing red…
you get the idea.

Monastery Visitor

A lady came to supper. The timid monks
restyled themselves and smiled into their lettuce,
giggled into Jell-o, squirmed like muffins
rising to a warmth of gentle grace.

Her glass soprano filtered through the bass,
rang out like glitter, silver on the tough ones
used to brawn, fragility a menace
locked with sweethearts' photos in attic trunks.

Bright fingernails on thick china trap
a wonder wide, their eyes too big for sockets.
The countess bows her auburn hair above

potato soup while chastened hearts like taps
release their evening prayer from sleeve and pocket
over roast beef getting cold for love.

Think About It

The best gifts
come unaware—
summer storms
and cancer.

The Soft Spot That Will Not Heal

In the kitchen somewhere
behind the pots,
find the marble cutting board.

Run your finger on the surface
where the turkey slices used to fall
and gravy seeped into the crevices.

Where you least expect it,
hidden under color,
the stone will give

beneath your touch,
a softness in the slab,
a secret from the ages.

Once you've found it,
it is yours—never will
the quiet distance be the same.

When out of the darkness
the board appears for service,
holiday or not, you'll know

here's a sermon that never quits,
a mother throbbing in her grave,
a lover more reluctant than most,
a story that won't go away.

Autumn

I trim the garden hoping
to stave the winter off.
I may as well pretend
the gold and amethyst
falling at my boots
is worth the effort.

They're not. The brown
succeeding them is every bit
as beautiful as what
the purple summer brought,
festooning us, the royalty
we like to think we are.

But here come the mums,
all cushiony, all plush,
a first reminder death swings
around the corner,
snapping his finger
as the last roses fade.

Art Responds to Artist

Like God he scoops a hand in softened mud,
retrieves a lump, and squeezes water out,
unleashing dormant molecules surprised
they should be chosen for creative form.

The wheel spins, and what was shapeless crud
assumes a stance, impels a base and spout
toward elegance. His wetted thumbs surmise
dirt yearns to be a pot, fulfill a norm,

but every atom bristles into act,
resists the ordinary plan, and fights
to be unique. He gels a new design

to satisfy creator and the fact,
accepting what the clay defends and rights:
"I can accept your art if you do mine."

Carnival Animals

Imprisoned in the glass, they stare at us:
the one-eyed peacock guarding his ribbed urn,
the lions circling on their hamster wheel,
and panthers, mirrors of their royal selves.

The mousy kittens eat without a fuss,
awaiting children. Peter Rabbits yearn
for freedom, but they know their fate is sealed.
The swan just glides along on rainbow shelves.

Down under, where the kookaburra thrives,
we laugh at kangaroo and emu while
the magpie masquerades a parson bird.

This zoo in color thrills our lives,
as moving bowl to bowl and style to style,
we hear them sing and roar without a word.

Pseudodoxia Epidemica

His brain's as clean as an empty room
where dust never settles
because there is no dust,

where angels whirl in constantly
with their rick-racks of information,
none of it his.

A huge process-mill, the neurons grind
bits of arcane data daily,
invisible to anyone who stops to shop.

Because there is no truth, he never minds
the heady swing of pert philosophies
that wander from their corners, mix, and die.

It is the most amazing box of tricks
you'll ever see, and so we all return
time after time for each compulsive show.

Celestine Invicta

You have seen the Mississippi bluffs
tight against the winter ice and snow
holding grizzled roots deep in fissures.
No storm deracinates those fingers
reaching deep to prehistoric crevices.

You have seen the eagles to a hundred
generations, locking amorous grips
high above the greenery and tumbling
for the ecstasy of wonder, dreams of catfish
gone for the clutch of claw and feather.

You have seen the trees festooned in white
and pink, their glories crowned in red,
maroon and sweet Franciscan brown,
watching ages pass and ages birth,
too grand to snap in winter storms.

And you have seen the sliding river,
ever ancient, ever new, a goddess
bringing life and taking life, carve
a winding path no banks can hold,
a woman undeterred by law or expectation,
answering to her heart, her heart alone.

Gram

Fused into a wheel chair, she reigns,
body streaked with strained carrots
rejected from a plastic spoon.

Her fading brain filters to her fingers
picking forever at the linen rags
that bind her bones to metal rods and wheels.

Everywhere she drags herself,
she smells of last night's urine,
one beady hazel eye shaving visitors.

In the nurses' cage the charts,
impeccably clean and neatly inked,
diagram her classic curve to vegetable.

But some days her feet activate the dirty floor,
and all the surge of spicy mineral
rejuvenates her brittle stalk to green.

She spits a yellow juice
while orderlies applaud her will to live:
our springtime queen, our Gram.

We Release You

I will not judge your going nor expect
answers from a world inclined to gape.
Better to accept what pilgrims may reject:
the last mirage, a soul anticipating rape.

It is enough to know your shell has cracked
and finalized your stop, remind the crew
that this oasis recently was sacked:
witness the waste of grapes, the rind of honeydew.

Get past this pause, ignore the dancing girls,
the yogurt pans, the cakes of beaten wheat,
your only clue the dust that darkly whirls
pursuing musty tracks from camel feet.

Happy Times

Another American boy was killed in Iraq
the day of Jenna Bush's wedding.
He really wanted to be there, in Crawford,
among the Texas mesquite and the prickly pear,

but the bullets fractured his face,
splattered his eyes and nose across
the concrete wall he was defending
for Halliburton from the infidel.

Meanwhile the rose punch flowed
Crawford-style with orange slices floating
in the champagne foam, and guests,
sweating in the springtime Texas sun,

complained about the heat, the flies,
the inconvenience of dust and sticky burrs.
Life is never easy—not at weddings,
not on killing fields. Everybody suffers.

The Methodist Way

A mountain has a certain silence even
when the winter ice ravages its
great face. It simply sits and lets the roaring
tear its wrinkles, rip into its pores.

You'd think that spring would bring among the leaves
a sighing rustle of relief, and yet
the mountain sits and watches, boring
every bobolink, expecting more.

So you arrive with summer, sitting proper,
pert in your religious wicker chair,
and rarely clear your throat or anxious brain,

content to wait for autumn when your hope,
precise as clockwork, can adjust its tune
to study cycles, breathe a hymn again.

Office Visit

As I talked to her
about the Peace Corps,

she looked at me
with anxious brown eyes

and wound her hair
into a chignon

which she fixed
with a kitchen spoon.

Pieta

She clutches broken guts
against her silver mantle,
all his godness gone.

What were his eyes are fleshy eggs,
what were his hands are birds
flown south and west.

Nothing nests inside that tired heart,
no pearl pink cockatoo intent
to break through bland and crippled skin,

the shadow of a man,
hushed, shelled, poured out,
a seamless gush of wonder.

Eggs for Show

When he dragged the crate
out of the dead fireplace, you'd think
they'd never seen an egg before,

but there they were cooing over
rhea (the green one) and ostrich,
all manner of fragile homes.

They didn't care a fig about the broken hearts
of mothers who never got to hatch
their babies into Texas light

because the fashion gurus wanted shells
to grace their living rooms and dens
in Pflugerville and Wimberley.

So I'm left scowling out the window
while the manly guests engorge their thrills
rubbing shells between their thick paternal fingers.

You Put in the Commas

remembering that clutter builds in corners
on a shelf the yellow bowling shirt
your father wore on Tuesday nights
a dream as effervescent as the thought
to put on roller skates and fly again

there has to be a place for detritus
a burial ground where old elephants face
the glorious truth and fall knowing that
their friends and sisters will soon come
to sniff the body and think beautiful thoughts

no time to finish everything the brain claws at
the symphony in D and the perfect cheese soufflé
the glut of work that never seems to shrink
the nightmare of the young rising in their energy
to find your heap of poetry and burn it

at last the brain has had enough
and shuts a final door to consequence
sits looking back at good and bad
to sort irrelevance from understanding
there's slim difference between the two

A Lesson from the Dolphins

In 1649 the British finally got around
to killing Henry VIII. They thought
they were chopping Charles I's arrogant head
from his arrogant body, but they weren't:

it was the power-hungry prick of six wives
they pulled through the window of the banquet room
at Whitehall, pushed to his knees, delivered to
the executioner in a waiting sun.

Then all their agony of dissing the pope
and sucking Luther's tit came to a finale of blood
when the boy lay torsoed, and his life seeped
through make-shift boards to dirt below

where enterprising citizens sopped the drops
in cloth martyr style, little knowing
they worshipped a beast a century old
who was laughing at them from a cloud.

It's funny how history shoves our noses
into truth and laughs as we squirm in the mess
of our collected past. We spend our lucid hours
awash in what-was, steeped in every atrocity

of every Kahn and viceroy because the past
is the only thing we control or think we can.
We squeeze its details and derail its momentum,
using its contours to hide our ignorance.

Someday we'll forget what's done and ignore
what's-to-come. We'll live like dolphins for
what's now, our latest mate, the most recent wave,
the krill arriving from wherever. There is a bliss

in not knowing, when analysis stops the second before
and the second after, when we care nothing for anything
that isn't and live to enjoy the flesh of the moment
and the spirit of now, the magic of the infinite yes.

In the Garden

When Easter morning cracks Jerusalem sky
meridian-bound by hills run green and blue,
I come to find the dew-drenched garden by
lithe Cedron. A pink and creamy cockatoo
nudges me forward into lavender.

Unknown, unseen, in the morning breeze,
I watch the flowers fight to break the womb.
I stalk the gardener. Purple knees
of pharisaic bloodroot rise to bloom
up amber glassy in the early rays.

The rock nearby, its bloody tarnished face
disdaining cheerless mourners from The Skull,
exhausted all. In time, the chartered race.
Today the pause. Our lives enjoy no lull
when women rave in aloetic dreams.

I see an emptied alabaster tomb
in air as richly borne by hyacinth
as columbine. But why the barren room?
Sir, your burnished clothes belie the scent:
gardenia and rose.

Mary, Mary, quite contrary,
what in the garden glows?

Revolution

1. Louis

The horror lingers centuries after
pitchforked women marched
Versailles to Paris, pulling the royal family
back to their mad fates.

The ladies would not dignify
their king by title at his trial:
it was "Louis Bourbon"
in the docket, in the tumbrel,

strapped to the wooden bed
of the merciful guillotine
that whisked him off
into fleur-de-lis clouds.

2. Robbespierre

When Erisichtheus turned on itself,
the dapper Robbespierre,
who dressed quietly,
lived close to the bone,

milked his brain for the Revolution,
was tied, broken wristed, screaming in pain,
to the nasty slab of wood and left
facing a cheerless Paris sky.

Today little French boys,
sopping up the broken pieces
of various bodies
and in various baskets

various heads,
still revere his facile mind
of rhetorical flourish.
Who will ever sort it out?

3. Charlotte

She said she killed one man
to save a hundred thousand,
she and her knife hidden
underneath a flowered scarf.

Women should thank her too
for bringing Marat his due—
serves him right receiving
ladies while in his tub.

So who gets to be painted
by David? The butcher
in the water. And Miss Corday?
Baudry did it right for her.

But guillotined, she got a slap
from the executioner Legros
on her dead cheek. And Baudry?
Three months in jail.

Poets for James Merrill

As water tightened into ice for winter,
where amber hardened into gold from summer,
dirt and taproots pack to form in spring
what later peak for harvest in the fall.
So early in our rose-poetic morning
we grind to life what mind has saved from night.

Nothing grows out of a loveless night—
cocoons dry up as easily in winter
as when July remembers of a morning
that sleeping worms should die defying summer
if they hang in dreams of mums for fall
or delay their resurrection until spring.

Intensities that aggravate and spring
to sticky coils cooled by jealous night
can learn a lesson from September's fall
of sweet peas: melodies released in winter
blister in a wind that only summer
can enjoy. Unless some golden morning

tame the snow, shackle it for morning,
charm its crystals to engorge a spring
that should by law be frozen until summer
sign its brokered lease, the purple night
will claim the better part of life for winter,
stake its ground where ribboned petals fall.

You see, if anything or something, fall
is nothing but a eunuch for the morning
birthed by all the calm surprises winter
saves to catch the early things of spring.
Whatever hates to wait can brave its night
pretending what's out there is really summer.

68

Some poets ripen into color. Summer
makes them hard, cauterized for fall,
and all the venom secreted by night
perfects their beauty. Any given morning
marigold, gloxinia, lilies spring
to stiff attention, half suspecting winter.

Your readers thaw that winter, and the summer,
calcified from spring, endures for fall.
If you sing morning, they can weather night.

Parade

Stop!!
The parade is on its way
and already in the air
is the whistle and the toot
of the first big band
but first of all the mayor's car
and uncles cousins brothers mothers
all wrapped in a big fat sedan
followed by the fire trucks
and noise without end
from sirens shrill
while clanging bells
pass Dante's hells
in sheer strife for havoc on the ear.

Cousin Peggy, hurry up,
you gonna miss the first float
here it comes—
palm trees and pretty girls
waving in the summer heat
and roses mums pom-pons
in tiers of gold
surmounted by a queen
LOOK!!
the queen is Auntie Emily
how'd the hell'd she get on there?
She's got bow legs.
She must know the druggist.
Aunt Emmy, Emmy,
throw me a flower
Aunt Emmy, Emmmmmmmyyyyy
oh, you stupid bum
you stepped right on my toe
watch where you're goin'

rum pum rum pum
rum pa pa rum pum
rum pum pum pum
rum pa pa rum

Stop!!
The first band is passing by
in suits of green
and red flags
lots and lots of red flags
one two three four
one two three four
play a song
play a song for us
play a song
play a song

rum pum rum pum
rum pa pa rum pum
rum pum pum pum
rum pa pa rum

Now little scouts
and big scouts
and lots and lots of middle scouts
boy scouts
girl scouts
row after row
troop one troop two
green and blue
troop nine troop ten
aren't they ever gonna end?
I'm bored.

Aunt Jo, where's the lemonade?

Wait!!
Here come some more floats
this one's throwing loaves of bread
this one beads and that one red
miniature atom bombs filled with candy
Who's the wiseacre?
Get outta my way

No thanks no lemonade

Ooh, lots of clowns
funny clowns
and more floats and shiny bands
with clarinets in gloved hands
horns and pipes
drums and fifes

I don't want any lemonade

floats and floats
bands and bands
round the corner
my lands it's Amy on that float
Hi Amy hi
toss me a flower
got it touché!
paper mache?

Aunt Jo, I think I will have some lemonade.

rum pum rum pum
rum pa pa rum pum
rum pum pum pum
rum pa pa rum

Portrait

Since autumn chestnuts fallen from the trees
have pocked the lawn and stopped the swinging gate
from sudden shoves, frustrating every breeze,
we know at last November comes too late,
that spring was here and summer came for lunch,
but early twilight hopes the winter be
announced by bittersweet, and so a bunch
rejuvenates our table set for tea.
Two lumps submerged in each enameled cup
do much to make the drink endurable.

"Tea," her fingers draw the saucer up,
"has never dulled your soul. You're curable,"
(dark visions of myself a swinging ham)
"but for myself the past is never gone."
She stalls, her muffin trimmed with peach-quince jam.

I wish I were a quince and not the pawn
she forwards inch by inch to boring death.
Cacophonous her laughter cools the tea
and ricochets. Her breathing sugared with
the honeyed spreads begins to sicken me.

"Plato, you know—at least you told me so—
Plato believed that all things have been tied
down here to things above and form a row
from here to some pre-life of life supplied,
or some such thing—you never were too clear."

I don't look up but smile down through the tea
and find the steam, more than herself, comes near
the truth: on smoking upward from the knee
it fogs the eye and passes by the brain
to regions where transcendence holds a key.
True steam recounts to me what they sustain—
those lands where truth is truth and tea is tea.

My eyes dissolve, I'm lost to her again,
but summer reveries no longer hold
me tight. I wake to watch her scratch the wen
along her heirloom nose, a creamy gold,
and wonder, as she quickly finds her drink,
if something I have said has made her change
to erudition recently: to think
that she can think is new, unsettling, strange.

"You rarely come to see me anymore—
you college boys are nearly all the same.
Remember when you first approached my door?
Behind that drape I watched you as you came."

What can I say to excavate the truth?
That I knew that she hid behind the lace?
Her one disguise is vapored in vermouth
whenever she smiles wrinkles through her face.
Her question hangs: she offers me a tart.
Refused, she ebbs, attacks it with a knife.
Yes, old you are, old dame, though young in heart,
but heart is only half the tale of life.

"You used to tell me all about yourself,
your weird ideas, fears. With some success
I'd try to worry for your mental health.
I'm past that now. You see, I do progress."

I'm not so sure of that but force a nod.
The million little things she says go by
without a comment.

"We even spoke of God
and then your thoughts were tasteless more than dry.
You always seem so serious. Anyway
I always welcomed Plato's thoughts as best.
His world somewhere of pure ideas may
remain for me more luscious than the rest
of all your silly theories." Another tart
falls victim to her lips and yellow teeth.
"You often think with this," she taps her heart,

entwines her fingerends into a wreath,
and then assumes a knowing air: "That place
which Plato claimed to be before we were
had correspondences that space by space
are imaged in all things that here occur."
Her sweeping hand outlines the room and stops,
a spreading mouth subtends her eyes, she laughs,
(her hand stays poised above the lemon drops)
"Your neck must correspond to some giraffe's!"

I seek a refuge in my cup. My eyes
pretend to miss her joke. Though in her wart
lies repartee (the wart demands by size
an elephant), I cancel my retort.
She creases into silence, and the day,
remembering that autumn lives for night
has gathered up its light where tea things lay
and creeps across the window out of sight.

The time has come to leave. I only came
four years ago because I thought I knew
how I could use her. Then she learned my game.
I rise. She takes the cup: "I'll write to you."

She must have sensed that somehow it must end
so this cliché, much softer than some other,
could buffet like a pillow and could send
me on my way more gently than another.
I reach the door and turn for one last look—
the marble eyes and sad vermouth will know
I've gone, some day, and like a child's book
am closed. I crush the chestnuts as I go.